100

I Love You's

By

Jera Sky

JeraSky.com

INTRODUCTION

I wanted to write this book to help others express to those they love how much they love them when they can't find their own words.

These are all my I love you's to someone I love very much.

DEDICATED TO

H.D.A

TABLE OF CONTENTS

I DIDN'T FALL FOR YOU.

YOUR SPIRIT + MINE
WERE ALREADY ONE BEFORE.
I WAS REMINDED OF IT WHEN
OUR EYES LOCKED.

THE LIGHT OF 1,000 SUNS

COULDN'T WARM ME AS MUCH

AS YOUR MORNING SMILE

:)

I EXPECTED LESS

THAN I DESERVED

EVERY DAY

UNTIL THE DAY

I KISSED YOU.

IT'S LIKE YOU'RE THE

LITTLE BLANKET

THAT KEEPS MY HEART

SAFE AND WARM

EVERY NIGHT

I ENJOY THE

PRESENCE OF YOU

WITH THE SOFT SMELLS OF

LAVENDER AND CROISSANTS

IN THE MORNING. SUN

THE STAINED GLASS COLOR OF
YOUR EYES LEAVE ME
BREATHLESS EVERY TIME THEY
SHINE INTO MINE.

YOUR SMILE FILLS MY
SOUL LIKE THE HAPPINESS
I GET FROM A GUMBALL
MACHINE ON A LONG
ROAD TRIP.

LIKE A DEVIL'S KISS

ROSE WATER DRIPS

TWO BECOME ONE

I DREAMT OF YOU

FOLLOWING THROUGH TIME

SO I COULD SEE YOU CLEARLY

AND HOLD YOU CLOSE

IN MY MIND DEARLY

LIPS, NOSE, EYES

WE ALL HAVE
BUT ONLY SHE

GIFTED YOU YOURS
TO THAT WHICH

I ENJOY

MOST

A BLACK HORSE

A WHITE HORSE

CHARGING FORTH

BOUND BY MAGIC

WITHOUT THE OTHER

THEY CEASE TO EXIST

11

IN ALL THE DAYS WE'VE SPENT
AWAY I'VE TATTOOED YOU ON
THE INSIDE OF MY MIND. WHEN
I WAKE YOU'RE ALWAYS
THERE EVEN WHEN YOU'RE NOT.

HURDLING THROUGH SPACE
EVERY TIME I REACH MY
ASTRONAUT HAND OUT FOR HELP
YOUR HAND IS THE ONLY
ONE THAT APPEARS FOR ME

WE'RE TWO RARE FLOWERS

BLOOMING AT THE SAME TIME

UNDER THE FULL MOON

ONCE IN A LIFETIME

IN AS LIGHTNING TURNS

SAND TO GLASS, YOU'VE

TURNED ME TO PURE BLISS

BLUE FIRES BLAZING

LIGHTNING STORMS

TWISTED TORNADO WINDS

HELD IN A LITTLE GLASS BOTTLE

THAT BOBS IN THE OCEAN

CHAOS AND PEACE

TOGETHER WE BALANCE

I HOPE YOU FEEL THE ESSENCE

OF EVERYTHING WONDERFUL IN

EVERY HUG I GIVE TO YOU

BECAUSE IT'S WHAT YOU'VE ALWAYS

GIVEN TO ME.

IN EVERY LEAF I AM REMINDED

OF THE GREEN OF YOUR EYES AND

STRANGERS WALK FAR AWAY

FROM ME AS I STARE

LOVINGLY INTO A FACE FULL

OF SUGAR MAPLE LEAVES.

THE SPACE BETWEEN MY HEART
AND MOUTH OF WHICH ALL
MY WORDS GET STUCK IS
FILLED WITH THE MOST
BEAUTIFUL WORDS I HAVE NOT
YET WRITTEN FOR YOU. ALWAYS
THERE, ALWAYS FULL, ALWAYS
DANCING AROUND WAITING TO
SURPRISE YOU.

I FEEL THINGS I'VE NEVER

EVEN BEEN ABLE to IMAGINE

FEELING WHEN I WALK

TOWARDS YOU.

HAMMOCK LINE TATTOOS

AFTER NAPS WITH YOU

ARE THE MOST DELIGHTFUL

FEELING UNDER MY

FINGERS

YOU'RE BOTH THE ONE WHO

LEAVES ME BREATHLESS AND

REVIVES ME EVERY TIME

YOU WHISPER A GIGGLE

IN MY EAR.

YOU REACH DEEP INSIDE MY
SOUL AND HELP ME REMOVE
ALL THE PARTS OF ME
OTHERS HATED ME FOR.
THANK YOU FOR
LOVING ALL
OF ME.

You're the most amazing

person I could never

have dreamed up.

YOU ENHANCE EVERY PART

OF MY BEING EVERY TIME

I FEEL LIKE I FALL

SHORT.

YOU TESLA COIL MY INSIDES

WITH EVERY TOUCH, EVERY

GRASP, EVERY BRUSH OF

YOUR ARM ON MINE WHEN

WE WALK DOWN THE STREET.

YOU ARE THE STARS
THAT FILL MY
UNIVERSE

27

YOUR SLEEPY HALF AWAKE

KISSES TICKLE MY LIPS

LIKE BUTTERFLY KISSES.

THERE IS NO ONE I'D

RATHER BE QUESTIONING

EXISTENCE WITH THAN

YOU.

I HOPE TO BE PART OF
EVERY THING THAT REMINDS
YOU HOW MUCH OF A GIFT
TO THIS REALITY YOU
ARE.

THERE IS NO ME

WITHOUT YOU,

IN THE LEAST CODEPENDENT

WAY POSSIBLE.

LOL

EVERY LOVE SONG WAS WRITTEN

ABOUT YOU AND I WISH I

COULD GIVE THEM ALL TO YOU

AS IF THEY WERE FROM MY

OWN MAKING.

YOU ARE LIKE A BREATHTAKING
SUNSET I STOP MY DAY
FOR TO ENJOY AND WATCH
AS IT UNFOLDS INTO
EVERYTHING PERFECT
IN THIS WORLD.

♥

IN A FIELD OF
        THOUSANDS OF BLOOMED

FLOWERS

        AS I STARE ABOUT

NOTHING ISMORE BREATH-

(((((GASP)))))

- TAKING

        THAN YOU MY

        LOVE.   ♥

34

YOU

JUST YOU

AND ME

FOREVER

WRAPPED UP TIGHT
  IN THE EARLY MORNING LIGHT

THE SUN FALLS UPON YOUR CHEEK

AS A TEAR FALLS UPON MINE

  NEVER IN MY LIFE
HAVE I FELT MORE GRATEFUL

  FOR ALL THAT IS

BECAUSE WITH YOU

  EVERYTHING MATTERS

THE SOUND OF YOUR VOICE

DANCES INSIDE OF ME

AND TICKLES ALL THE PARTS

NO ONE HAS EVER

TOUCHED

MY MOUTH ACHES

FROM SMILING

SO MUCH

EVERY TIME

YOU ARE AROUND

DECORATED LIKE SUGAR COOKIES

IN A GOURMET BAKERY

YOU WET MY MOUTH WITH DESIRE

AT THE MERE SIGHT OF YOU.

WANTING THE BEST ONE, THE ONE
THAT WAS ALREADY MINE BEFORE
WE EVEN KNEW EACH OTHER
EXISTED

HOPELESS ROMANTIC.
HOPELESS ROMANTIC.
HOPELESS ROMANTIC.

THEN I MET YOU.

HOPEFUL ☺ HAPPY ROMANTIC.

T-SHIRTS ON THE FLOOR.

I WANT TO SHOW YOU

ALL OF MY NAKED.

THE OUTSIDE OF COURSE

BUT MORE IMPORTANTLY

THE INSIDE I'VE ONLY EVER

SHARED WITH MYSELF.

SPEAK TO ME
THE WAY YOU WOULD

A FAIRY IN THE WOODS,

LIKE NO ONE YOU'VE
EVER MET BEFORE

AND I'LL DO THE
SAME
FOR YOU

WITH YOU I'M NEVER

WITHOUT THE BUILDING

BLOCKS FOR OUR

BRIGHT FUTURE TOGETHER.

IT'S LIKE THE SUPPLIES ARE

FREE AND THE WORLD IS OURS

FOR THE MAKING

DREAM, DRIP, DRIZZLE

EVERY   EXCLAIMS

FUTURE   FIREFLIES

GORGEOUS   GRATITUDE

HAPPINESS   HURDLES   HUMBLE

INQUISITIVE   INKS

JUXTAPOSED   JOKERS

KIND   KISSES

LEVELING   LIQUIDS

MAKE ME MARRY

SPARKLING SPIN CYCLED
ENERGY MOVES
ME JOYOUSLY INTO
EVERY NEW DAY
WITH YOU

I CAN'T BELIEVE YOU EXIST!

I CAN'T BELIEVE I EXIST!

I CAN'T BELIEVE WE EXIST
TOGETHER!

SHHH... DON'T TELL ANYONE

IT'S OUR SECRET MAGICAL

WIND CHIME

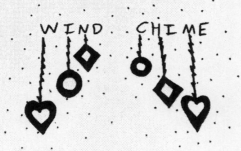

THE ONLY ONE WHO
    COULD LIGHT THE
INFINITE BURNING TORCHES

LEADING THE PATH
    TO EVERY PART OF ME

SINGING BOWLS SOUND
WHEN YOU'RE NEAR
ALL THE DARK CALLOUSED PARTS
THAT OTHERS LEFT BROKEN
WE HEAL EACH OTHER
LOVING ALL THE PARTS OTHERS TOLD US
WEREN'T GOOD ENOUGH
WE KNOW THERE IS NO ONE BETTER

WE WERE MADE FOR EACH OTHER
IN EVERY WAY

THE LOVE I HAVE FOR YOU

TAKES OVER EVERYTHING

LIKE THE HOT LAVA FROM

A NEWLY ERUPTED VOLCANO.

EVERYTHING IN MY WAKE

FUSES WITH LOVE.

NEVER THE SAME.

NEVER SEPARATED.

I PROMISE TO CHERISH EVERY
DAY WITH YOU. THE BAD
ONES MOST OF ALL BECAUSE
ITS THE TIME I'M CLOSEST TO
LOSING YOU AND I WANT ALL
THE DAYS WITH YOU, NOT JUST
SOME OF THEM.

I ALWAYS THOUGHT MY HEART

WAS MY OWN TO GIVE UNTIL I

MET YOU AND FOUND OUT YOUR

HEART WAS MINE AND MINE WAS

YOURS. ALWAYS ENTWINED.

THE WAYS YOU FEEL ABOUT ME,
THE WAYS YOU SEE ME,

THE WAYS I INSPIRE YOU,
THE WAYS I HELP YOU BE A BETTER YOU
ARE THE WAYS I FEEL ABOUT YOU,
THE WAYS I SEE YOU,
THE WAYS YOU INSPIRE ME

AND THE WAYS YOU HELP ME BE A
BETTER ME. IN EVERY
WAY YOU FEEL I DO TOO.

I LOVE YOU LIKE BREATHING.

I DO IT EFFORTLESSLY AND
WITHOUT THINKING BECAUSE IT
COMES NATURALLY AS LOVING
YOU IS ESSENTIAL TO MY
EXISTENCE.

You've chiseled your name all over my body and I couldn't be more proud to show it off because I wouldn't have it any other way.

THE WHOLE WORLD COULD GO
UNDER WATER AND THE ONLY
THING I'D BE WORRIED
ABOUT LOSING IS YOU.

I WOULD ACTUALLY
SHARE THE RAFT,
I'M JUST SAYING...

UNDER A HIGH NOON SUN

SWEAT DRIPS

DANCE STOMPS

LUSCIOUS LAUGHTER

FLOODS MY PUPILS

WHEN I WAKE

AND YOU'RE IN SIGHT

A GOOD YEAR OF WINE

HAS NOTHING

ON THE YEAR YOU

WERE CREATED.

A VAMPIRE STAKE TO THE

HEART THAT REVIVED ME

AND REVERSED ALL THAT HAD

LONG SINCE DIED

YOU'RE THE PIZZA TO

MY HUNGRY TUMMY.

PERFECT TOGETHER.

YOUR SMILE LIGHTS UP
THE DEEPEST DARKEST PARTS
OF ME.
I'M MUCH HAPPIER IN
THE LIGHT.

YOU KNOW WHEN YOU SEE A
VIEW AND YOUR JAW JUST
DROPS AND YOU CAN'T STOP SAYING
WOW?

THAT'S YOU, TO ME.

I ENJOY YOU AS MUCH AS

HOT CHOCOLATE AND S'MORES

AROUND A CAMPFIRE

IN FALL.

LIKE KEYS OF IVORY BELOW MY

FINGERS THE WAY I TOUCH YOU

FEELS EXCITING, DIFFERENT AND

YET FAMILIAR EVERY TIME.

THE FIRST FALL WIND AND
BRUSH OF DRIED LEAVES MEANS
MORE TIME BY THE FIREPLACE
SNUGGLED TIGHTER AND CLOSER
TO YOU EVERY DAY AS THE COLD
WINTER WEATHER APPROACHES.

I CANNOT HIDE ALL
THE THOUGHTS
THE WISHES
OF LIFE FOREVER
ENTWINED WITH

EVERY PIECE OF YOU.

EVERY DAY HAS FELT LIKE A

DREAM SINCE LOVING YOU

ALL OF THE IMPOSSIBLE THINGS

I NEVER THOUGHT I'D BE ABLE

TO DO, HAVE BEEN MADE POSSIBLE

THANKS TO YOU

JUST BEING YOU.

IN THE TIMES WHEN I FEEL

THE WORST YOU HOLD ME

AS TIGHT AS YOU CAN AND SAY

"WE'LL MAKE IT THROUGH THIS"

I KNOW NO ONE

UNDERSTANDS ME

BETTER THAN YOU.

You knock the wind out of me
So I play dead

Til you come
Give me mouth to mouth

Works every time

BLESS ME WITH THE REST

OF YOUR KISSES AND

I'LL BLESS YOU WITH

THE REST OF MINE.

BREATHE INTO ME

WE KISS

THE AIR THATS BEEN THROUGH

YOU

RUNS THROUGH ME

BRINGS ME LIFE

I'D DRIVE TO THE ENDS OF
   THE WORLD
DIVE THE DEEPEST PARTS OF
   THE OCEAN
CLIMB THE TALLEST PEAKS

FLY TO THE EDGE OF SPACE
      FOR YOU
   OVER AND OVER

SMILE

RAISES EYEBROW

TONGUE BITE

WINK

ALL THE THINGS

I WANNA DO TO YOU

LiKE FLOWERS ON A
HiLLSiDE
MY BODY SWAYS BACK
AND FORTH
AS YOU NEAR

MY HEART PUMPS LIKE
A FLASH FLOOD

IS ABOUT TO GO DOWN

WHEN YOU'RE AROUND

EVERYTHING AROUND DIMS
AWAY BECAUSE YOU
ARE THE BRIGHTEST
LIGHT TO MY LIFE

I DIDN'T BELIEVE IN
ANGELS UNTIL I MET
YOU
I HAD NEVER SEEN SO
MANY MIRACLES IN A
ROW AND NOW I DON'T
KNOW HOW I EXPECTED LESS
THAN A MIRACLE EVERY DAY
EVER.

I DECORATE THE
BEDROOM OF MY
MIND WITH ALL MY
FAVORITE MOMENTS WITH
YOU

STANDING OUT IN THE
POURING SUMMER RAIN

WASHING AWAY ALL THE BAD

WE LOOK IN EACH OTHERS EYES

AND ONLY SEE GOOD

IT DOESN'T MATTER WHAT

OBSTACLES APPEAR

WE MAKE IT THROUGH

EVERYTHING AND ANYTHING

OUR LOVE IS ETERNAL

WITH CICADAS SINGING

TALL GRASS HIDING CREATURES

OF THE NIGHT

OUT ON THE VERANDA

THE SUMMER SUN SETS

PAINTBRUSHES LEFT WET

FACE GRASPS

SOFT KISSES

EVERYTHING IS EVERYTHING

IS US

TIME WITH YOU

IS BETTER THAN

TIME WITHOUT YOU

ALL THE DAYS WITHOUT YOU
PREPARED ME FOR

ALL THE DAYS WITH YOU.
I GET TO BE THE BEST
ME FOR YOU
NOTHING SHORT OF
EVERYTHING YOU DESERVE.♥

SWEET NOTHINGS AND
SOMETHINGS AND
EVERLASTINGS

WITHOUT
EXCEPTION
OR
HESITATION

CURLED LIP SMILES

JOLT MY EVER BEATING

every time.

BOUQUETS OF LOVE

EVERY. DAY.

WRAPPED IN LACE

I'LL GRAB THE MACE

TO KEEP THE OTHERS AWAY

MY DIVINE

ONCE YOU WERE FOUND
NO QUESTIONS

MY LOVE IS ALWAYS
GIVEN

MIXTAPE RECORDS

SPINNING IN MY HEART

ALL THE SONGS YOU'VE

SELECTED — — —

LUMINESCENT SOUNDS

BRIGHTEN THE BALANCE

LET MY HEART BUBBLE

UP AND OVERFLOW A

RAINBOW

BRINGING PEACE

TO ALL THAT EVER WAS

YOU

ME

THIS BEAUTIFUL MAGNIFICENT
WORLD

WE WILL MAKE EVEN BETTER

THAN WE FOUND IT

IN EVERYTHING

WE CREATE TOGETHER

I DON'T NEED YOU IN THE
SENSE THAT I'm incomplete
without you...
I NEED YOU IN THE SENSE THAT
I NEED TO BE THE
ONE KISSING YOU AND TELLING
YOU THAT YOU'RE THE MOST
BEAUTIFUL PERSON EVERY
DAY :)

I'VE BEEN SEARCHING THE WORLD

FOR THE MOST PERFECT ROCK

FOR YOU

MY PENGUIN

IF I COULD BUY UP ALL
THE FLOWER BOUQUETS AND
GIVE THEM TO YOU

(WELL THAT'D BE A BIT SELFISH)

BUT THAT'D BE ONE
AMAZING DAY
OF THE MANY I'D LIKE
TO GIVE TO YOU

I FLY SO HIGH

TO THE SOUND OF THE RADIO

OVER OUR FAVORITE BRIDGE

I LOVE YOU LIKE A
SEAGULL LOVES STEALING
FOOD FROM PEOPLE ON
AN OCEAN PIER
       LIKE A BOSS

I AM GOING TO LOVE YOU
LIKE YOU'RE BRAND NEW
FULL OF EXCITEMENT
EVERY TIME I SEE YOU

I WOULD TRADE AS
MANY TIMELINES AS
I HAD TO
TO KEEP GETTING BACK
TO YOU

YOU INSPIRE ME TO TRY THINGS I
WOULDN'T HAVE OTHERWISE. YOU INSPIRE
ME TO BE A BETTER PERSON THAN I
WAS YESTERDAY EVERY DAY

YOU INSPIRE ME TO LOVE MORE

YOU INSPIRE ME TO CARE MORE ABOUT THE
THINGS I DO. YOU INSPIRE ME TO
CREATE. YOU ARE THE REASON I SHARE
SO MUCH OF MYSELF WITH THE WORLD.
YOUR "MISTAKES" INSPIRE THE BEST IDEAS
I'VE EVER HAD. **YOU** ARE MY
BIGGEST INSPIRATION

TO WHOM iT MAY CONCERN:

i LOVE YOU

I LOVE YOU

i love you

i love you

I Love You

i love you

THAT IS ALL.

I'LL LOVE YOU EVEN WHEN
YOU DON'T LOVE YOURSELF,

WHEN YOU'RE TOO HARD ON
YOURSELF. WHEN YOU'RE HIDING
YOURSELF AWAY
      YOU ARE EASY TO
        LOVE

I DON'T KNOW WHAT IN THE
HELL THE OTHERS WERE
THINKING.

I LOVE YOU LIKE THE WORLD

IS ABOUT TO END

OF EVERY SECOND
OF EVERY DAY

ABOUT JERA SKY

Just another being having a human experience on this flying rock through space.

Read more at amazon.com/author/jerasky

OTHER BOOKS BY JERA SKY

Should I Be Telling You This? (Poetry/Love)

Cosmos ii (Poetry/Love)

Cosmos of Constance (Poetry/Love)

Love Me Forever (Novel/Love)

100 Things To Get Rid Of (Minimalism/Self Help)

Can I Ask A Favor?

Thank you in advance for leaving a review on amazon if you enjoyed this book, were inspired by, found it useful or otherwise beneficial.

I greatly appreciate it!

amazon.com/author/jerasky

Thanks for your support and time!

You're awesome and I hope you have the best day!